WORLD WAR II
BROUGHT ADVANCES IN TECHNOLOGY

History Book 4th Grade

Children's History

Speedy Publishing LLC

40 E. Main St. #1156

Newark, DE 19711

www.speedypublishing.com

Copyright 2017

The main result of war is killing and destruction. It is not pretty or noble. However, out of the efforts nations made to win World War II came advances in many fields that help make our modern world possible. Let's find out about them!

WHAT WAR BROUGHT

Many things we depend on today, from the GPS on our phones to the microwave that heats our meals, use technology developed to help win World War II. The war showed humanity at its worst. Whole cities were set on fire. Two cities were destroyed by the most powerful weapon ever used. More than twenty million people died during the war, and many more suffered life-changing injuries.

7 days with Premium features are over
GO PREMIUM
Solebaystraat
s103
Livornostraat
Haarlemmerweg
Amsterdam
10:32
(3min)
1.9
km
43
km/h

PHONE GPS

WORLD WAR II RUINS

It does not set those horrors aside to note the many advances that also came out of the war. Sometimes they were accidental discoveries, sometimes one piece of a weapons system became useful in a different way altogether.

WEAPONS

Most of the countries that took part in World War II were still prepared to fight World War I, with a trench war on land and conflicts between battleships at sea. They had to upgrade very quickly after war broke out in 1939!

BATTLESHIPS

Fleets of battleships gave way to the power of aircraft carriers supported by fast destroyers, and submarines sneaking in to attack from underwater.

At the start of the war most tanks were heavy and slow moving castles designed to crawl over trenches and clear the way for infantry. By the end of the war the best tanks were lighter, faster, and equipped with more powerful and accurate cannons. They could attack an enemy position like cavalry, or dig in and be artillery support for an infantry attack. They were connected by radios, so all tanks could respond to a change in plans. Special tanks were created to "swim" to shore during an invasion, clear mine fields, or fire flames rather than cannon shells.

TANK

WARNING

"Smart" bombs could be aimed, and their track adjusted, by remote control.

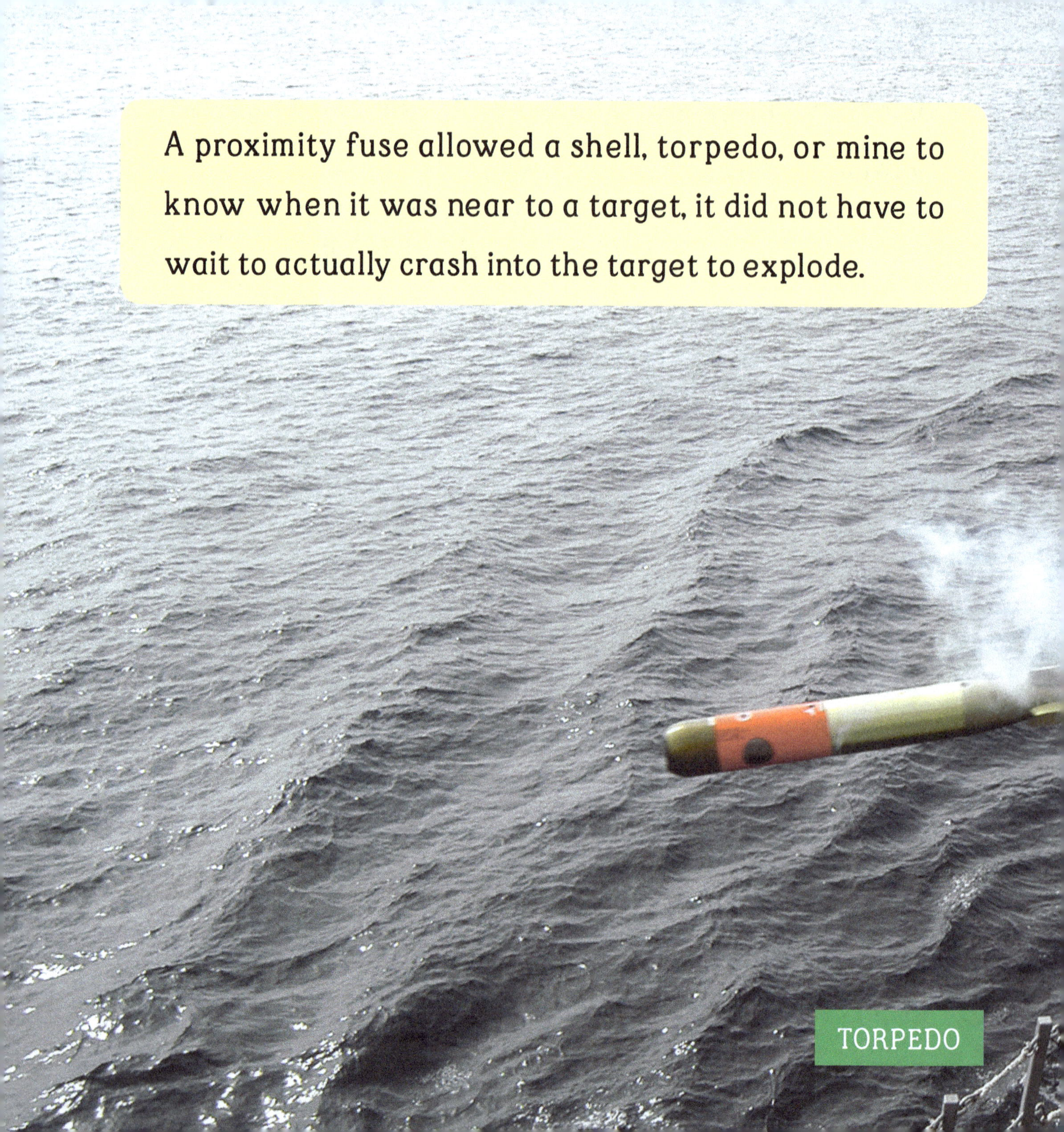
A proximity fuse allowed a shell, torpedo, or mine to know when it was near to a target, it did not have to wait to actually crash into the target to explode.

TORPEDO

Helicopters advanced from their infancy so they could take part in scouting, battles, and rescue missions.

The biggest weapon to come out of World War II, was the atomic bomb. The Great Britain and the United States combined forces to develop a successful bomb before anybody else. Using the bomb on two Japanese cities (Hiroshima and Nagasaki) ended the war a year or two earlier than might have been the case, and probably saved over two million lives, as Japan was prepared to fight to defend every square foot of its islands. Getting access to the power of the atom created a fearsome weapon, but it also opened the way to the development of nuclear energy for peaceful purposes.

ATOMIC BOMB EXPLOSION

WORLD WAR II

SYSTEMS

Huge efforts like an assault on a beach, or an attack on a city, required coordination of equipment, fighters, support people, doctors, ammunition, and much more. It was easy for an effort to collapse into a disaster. Out of the huge missions of World War II came a whole new field: project management. Almost all modern engineering, software development, or building project relies on the "best practices" developed by project managers.

At the start of the war, even the German army was not fully mechanized. It had powerful Panzer tanks, but it relied on mules pulling carts to bring ammunition and fuel to the tanks! Mechanization of systems, to speed creation and delivery of what the army needed, led after the war to vast improvements in construction, manufacturing, and even harvesting of crops, all around the world!

TANK

WORLD WAR II

EQUIPMENT

The range of problems requiring solutions in a war is endless. Here are some solutions that go on being useful in peacetime:

Hand-powered flashlight. The Philips Company in the Netherlands developed a lamp for soldiers. It had a handle you could squeeze to generate power that would light up the bulb. Crank-powered versions, that store a charge in the flashlight, are popular today with campers.

MECHANICALLY POWERED FLASHLIGHT

JERRYCANS
W↑D
1944

Jerrycan. This is container for carrying fuel or water. This was essential for supporting both troops and tanks when they operated far away from their storage areas. The cross design on the sides lets the can expand without splitting. Most people who go camping or have remote cabins rely on versions of the jerrycan to get liquids where they need them.

Artificial rubber and oil. Countries that could not get natural supplies of fuel and rubber for tires found ways to develop alternatives from chemicals. This led to inventions and discoveries that made a whole universe of plastic and synthetic goods possible.

TIRES

M&Ms CHOCOLATE

Candy-covered chocolate. Supplying compact energy to troops, and keeping up morale, was essential. The Mars Company discovered how to wrap chocolate in a hard sugar shell. This slowed down the melting of the chocolate in hot weather. The first M&Ms were made and sold only to the US Army for its troops. After the war, returning soldiers were the Mars Company's best customers!

FLIGHT

Airplanes came into their own as a fighting force in World War II. Fast, deadly fighters escorted slower, powerful bombers over enemy territory, where they would drop their payloads. Here are some of the advances to the world of flight that came out of the war:

FIGHTER AIRCRAFT

BUZZARDS
AV
AF 89 777
AV
AF 89 178

Pressurized cabins. If you fly at high altitudes you can avoid a lot of enemy gunfire. Pressurizing cabins let warplanes, and passenger planes after the war, fly higher and more quickly while keeping crew and passengers safer and in better comfort.

Radio navigation. Developing accurate navigation systems meant planes could get to their target even in bad weather with low visibility, and have a good chance of finding their way home again safely if they were not shot down. Navigation waves uses radio signals sent from towers at known locations. Combining the signals in a device on the plane showed where you were, and then you could figure out where you needed to go.

Peacetime use of systems like this is widespread. It helps pilots avoid obstacles and find the runway. It helps ship captains avoid colliding with other ships. Police forces use tools based on the same technology to check whether a car is speeding!

JET AIRCRAFT

Jet engines. By the end of World War II, the first jet-powered fighters were in use. They were far faster and more effective than any propeller-driven fighter plane. After the war, jet technology was quickly adapted for use in passenger planes and cargo flights.

ROCKETRY

Germany's V-2, or "vengeance weapon" was a cross between a guided missile and a remote-controlled aircraft. It killed thousands of people in the cities of Great Britain.

USA SPACE SHUTTLE

However, its technology was the basis of many advances:

- GPS systems like Google Earth.
- Satellite communications.
- Even space travel. The V-2 is the ancestor of every rocket that has taken off into space!

MEDICINE

In every war before World War II, as many people died from their wounds as died on the battlefields. People did not understand infection and how to prevent it, and had no idea of effects like Post Traumatic Stress Syndrome (PTSD) that can cripple a life or even cause a person to end it.

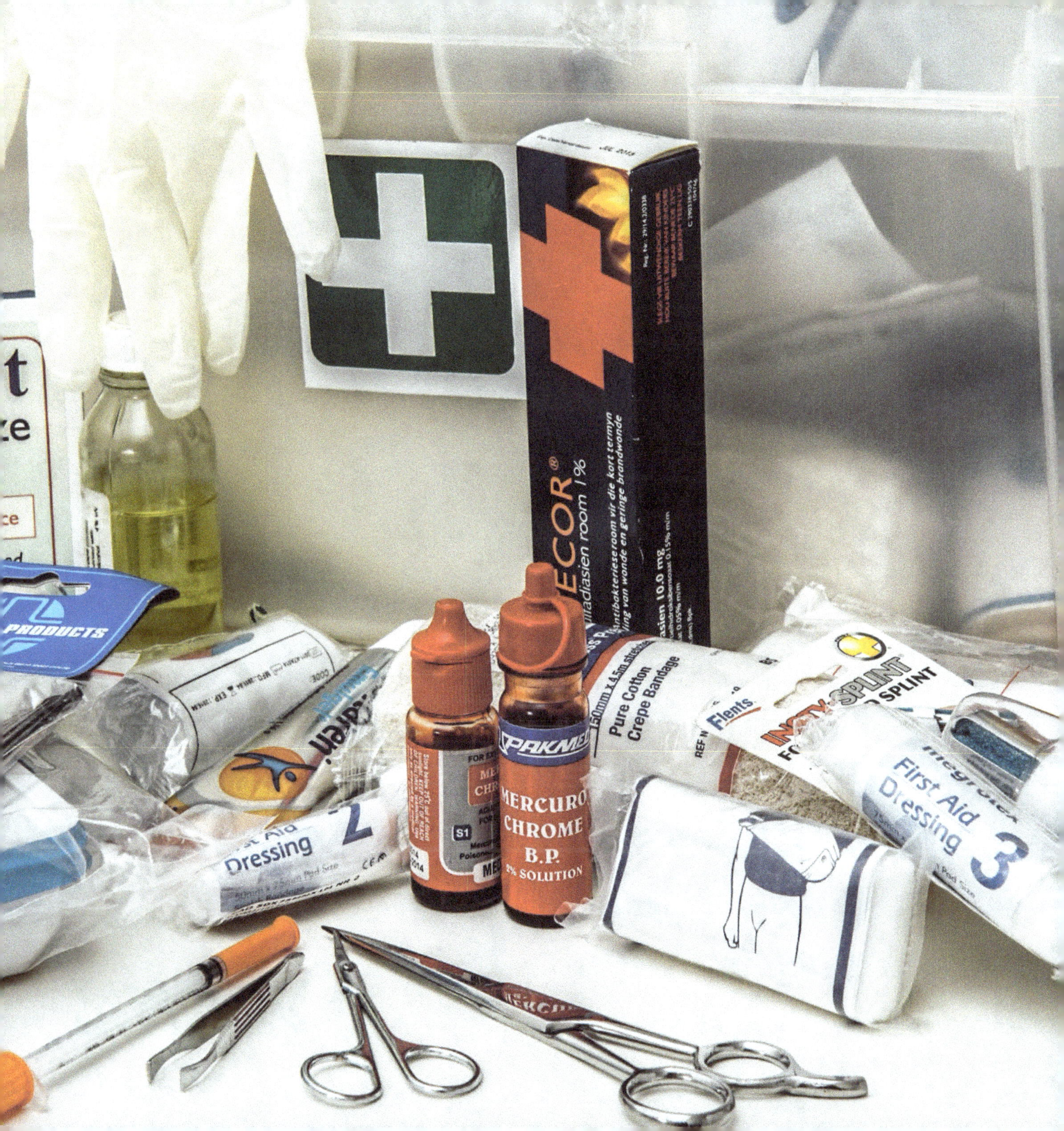
PRODUCTS
MERCOR
Antibakteriese room vir die kort termyn
behandeling van wonde en geringe brandwonde
FOR EXT
MERCURO
CHROME
B.P.
SOLUTION
S1
Pure Cotton
Crepe Bandage
Flents
REF N
INSTA-SPLINT
FOR FINGER SPLINT
First Aid
Dressing
First Aid
Dressing
2
First Aid
Dressing
3

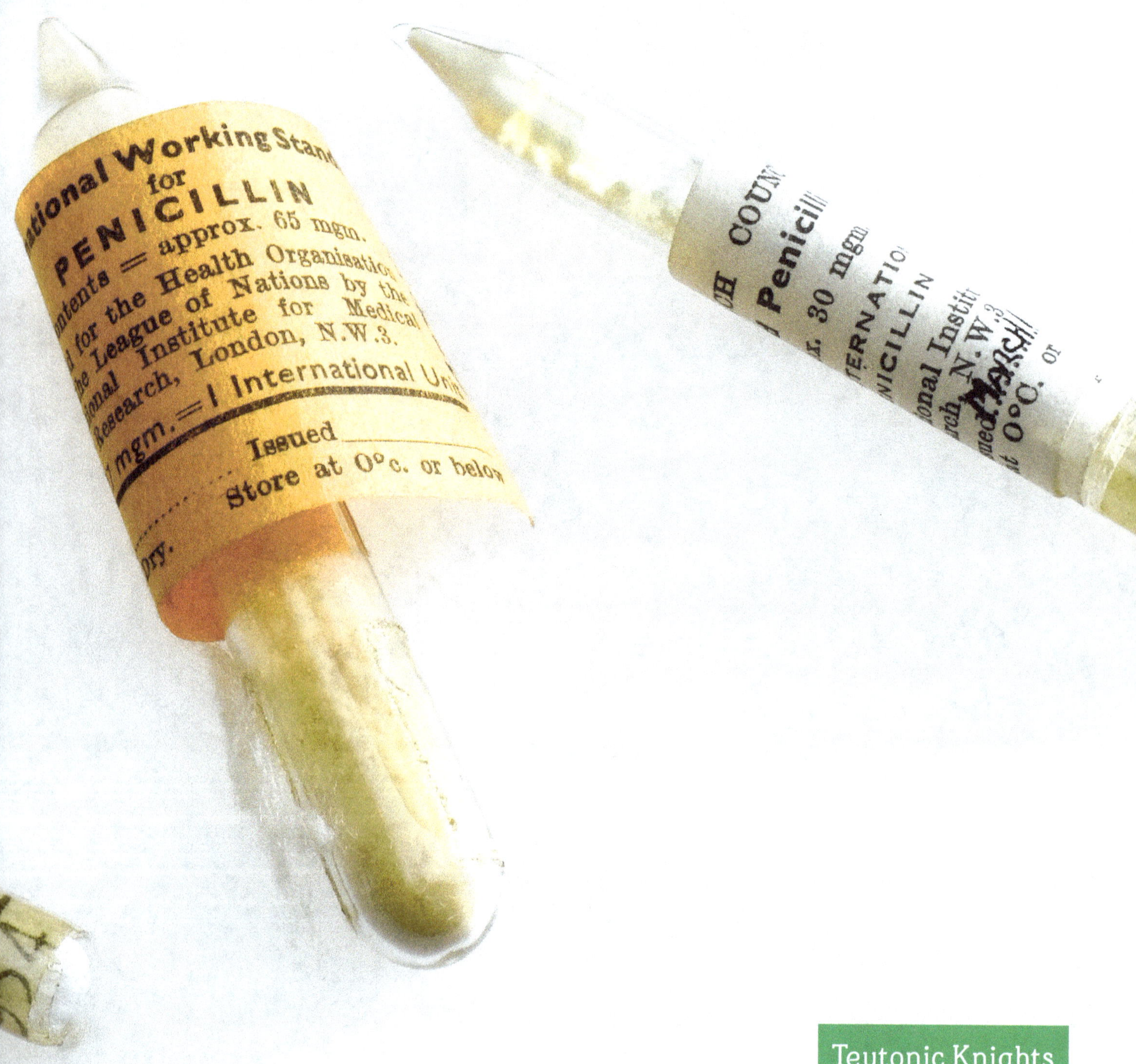

Teutonic Knights

Penicillin stands out as the poster child of medical improvements in World War II, although there were many other discoveries and new medicines. It had been discovered in 1928, but turning penicillin into a medicine and preparing it for use to fight infection and other diseases took until 1943. By 1944 the United States had produced over two million doses of penicillin, and its use saved the lives of as many as 15 percent of people wounded during the rest of the war.

COMPUTERS

Our whole world seems to run on computers now, but in 1939 they were in their infancy! The need to manage and organize large amounts of data forced huge improvements in computing and laid the groundwork for our modern information age. Now fire-control systems helped warships aim their guns faster and better so the shells they fired would get to their targets more often.

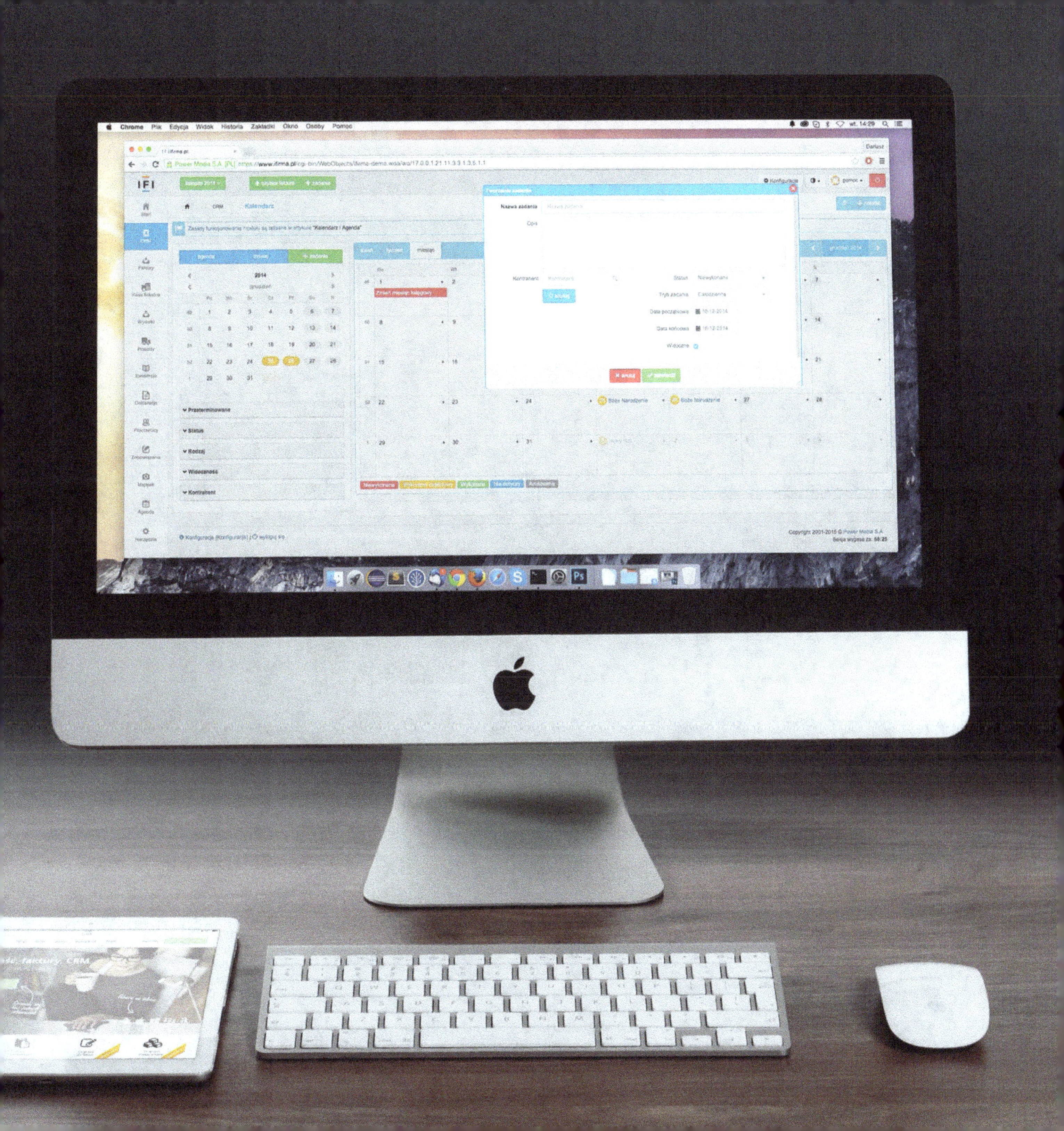
Chrome
Plik
Edycja
Widok
Historia
Zakładki
Okno
Osoby
Pomoc
IFI
Kalendarz
2014

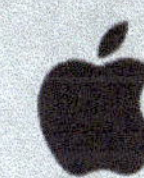

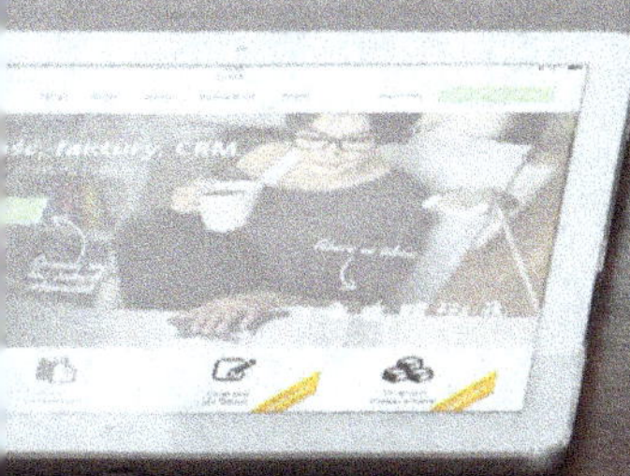

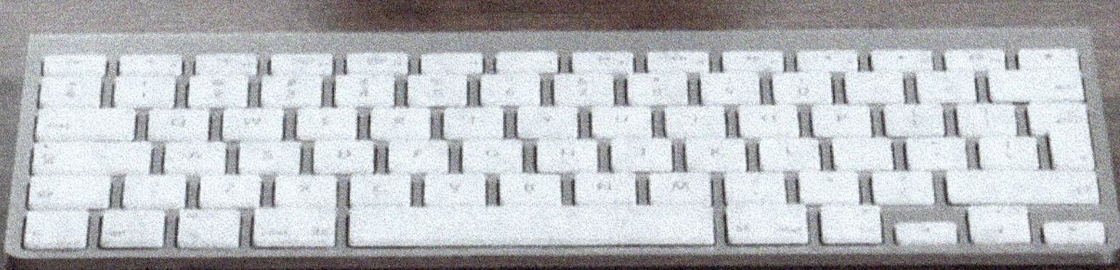

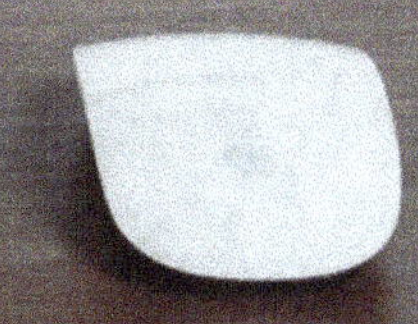

Germany developed programmable computers to develop designs for planes and guided missiles. These led to computer-assisted-design (or CAD) systems that architects and other designers use.

The Germans encrypted their messages before sending them, using a complex machine called Enigma. The British managed to break the code and gain access to the orders Germany was sending to its forces. This work led to developments in artificial intelligence and made possible much machine behavior that we take for granted now (electric-eye doors) or look for soon (self-driving cars)!

·1945·IWO JIMA·OKINAWA·KOREA·1950·
REVOLUTIONARY·WAR·1775–1783 ✕ FRENCH·NAVAL·WAR·1798–1801 ✕ TRIPOLI·1801–1805 ✕ WAR·OF·1812–1815 ✕ FLORI
UNCOMMON
VALOR
WAS A COMMON
VIRTUE
SEMPER
FIDELIS
THE U.S. MARINE CORPS WAR MEMORIAL

EVEN A WAR CAN PROVIDE GOOD THINGS

Wars are horrible and let out the worst instincts in people. But they also require bravery, persistence, loyalty, inventiveness, and foresight. Humans are good at fighting wars. Fortunately, we are even better at using our skills for peace!

Read about a soldier who found a better use for his skills in the Baby Professor book A Rich Man in Poor Clothes: the Story of St. Francis of Assisi.

Visit
BABY PROFESSOR
EDUCATION KIDS
www.BabyProfessorBooks.com
to download Free Baby Professor eBooks
and view our catalog of new and exciting
Children's Books